KT-226-337

How to Be a Scientist

# Analyse This!
## Understanding Scientific Enquiry

Susan Glass

**H** www.heinemann.co.uk/library

Visit our website to find out more information about Heinemann Library books.

To order:

📞 **Phone** 44 (0) 1865 888112

📠 Send a fax to 44 (0) 1865 314091

🖥 Visit the Heinemann bookshop at www.heinemann.co.uk/library to browse our catalogue and order online.

First published in Great Britain by
Heinemann Library, Halley Court, Jordan Hill,
Oxford OX2 8EJ, part of Harcourt
Education. Heinemann Library is a registered
trademark of Harcourt Education Ltd.

ⓒ Harcourt Education Ltd 2007
The moral right of the proprietor has been asserted.

All rights reserved. No part of this publication
may be reproduced, stored in a retrieval system, or
transmitted in any form or by any means, electronic,
mechanical, photocopying, recording, or otherwise,
without either the prior written permission of the
publishers or a licence permitting restricted copying
in the United Kingdom issued by the Copyright
Licensing Agency Ltd, 90 Tottenham Court Road,
London W1T 4LP (www.cla.co.uk).

Editorial: Nancy Dickmann and Rosie Gordon
Design: Victoria Bevan, Ron Kamen,
and AMR Design Ltd
Picture Research: Ruth Blair and Ginny Stroud-Lewis
Production: Camilla Crask
Originated by Chroma Graphics Pte. Ltd
Printed and bound in China by
WKT Company Ltd

10 digit ISBN 0 431 90677 7
13 digit ISBN 978 0431 90677 5
11 10 09 08 07
10 9 8 7 6 5 4 3 2 1

British Library Cataloguing in Publication Data

Glass, Susan
Analyse this! : understanding scientific enquiry. –
(How to be a scientist)
507.2

A full catalogue record for this book is available
from the British Library.

**Acknowledgements**

The publishers would like to thank the following
for permission to reproduce photographs: Alamy
Images pp. **38** (Chris Cameron), **42** (David Young-
Wolff), **5** (Holt Studios International Ltd), **40** (Juniors
Bildarchiv), **43** (Phil Degginger), **14** (Popperfoto);
Corbis pp. **4, 8, 9, 12, 18, 26,** Corbis/Bettmann, **6,
24**; Corbis pp. **7** (David Samuel Robbins), **11** (Denis
Scott), **27** (Karen Kasmauski), **28** (Owaki – Kulla),
**41** (Shift Photo/zefa); Frank Lane Picture Agency
p. **34** (S & D & K Maslowski); Getty Images pp. **15**
(Hutton Archive), **10** (Photodisc); Harcourt Education
pp. **34** (Ginny Stroud-Lewis), **16, 21, 21, 30,
33, 36, 36, 39** (Tudor Photography); Mary Evans
Picture Library pp. **13, 22;** NASA p. **19;** Photos.com
p. **31;** Science Photo Library pp. **23** (MARK THOMAS),
**29** (NASA).

Cover photograph: Getty Images/Taxi

The publishers would like to thank Bronwen Howells
for her assistance in the preparation of this book.

Every effort has been made to contact copyright
holders of any material reproduced in this book. Any
omissions will be rectified in subsequent printings if
notice is given to the publishers.

**Dedication**

I would like to thank my husband, John, for all his
help and encouragement. I want to dedicate this book
to him, my parents, my children Joanna, John, Billy,
and Tricia, and my granddaughter Madison.

**Disclaimer**

All the Internet addresses (URLs) given in this book
were valid at the time of going to press. However,
due to the dynamic nature of the Internet, some
addresses may have changed, or sites may have
changed or ceased to exist since publication. While
the author and publishers regret any inconvenience
this may cause readers, no responsibility for any such
changes can be accepted by either the author or
the publishers.

# Contents

Some words are shown in bold, **like this**. You can find out what they mean by looking in the glossary.

# Yellow fever

During the Spanish-American War in Cuba in 1898, yellow fever killed thousands of American soldiers. The US Army called in the doctor and scientist Walter Reed and his team to stop this terrible disease.

Yellow fever was given its name because its victims turned yellow before they died. Many doctors and scientists believed it spread by contact with an infected person's clothes or bedding, but nobody knew for sure.

A scientist named Carlos Finlay thought mosquitoes were responsible for spreading the disease. He believed that after mosquitoes bit a sick person they could spread the disease by biting other people.

## The investigation

Walter Reed started his scientific investigation with the question, "How is yellow fever spread?" Two possible answers were mosquitoes or contact with a sick person's clothes and bedding. He and his team set up two **experiments** to test these answers.

Here, yellow fever patients are cared for in a US Army hospital during the Spanish-American War in 1898.

Mosquitoes can pass on disease when they bite a healthy person after they have bitten a sick person.

Reed had two small houses built so that no mosquitoes could get in them. He had dirty bedding and clothes from yellow fever victims brought into one house. Three brave volunteers spent 20 days there, wearing the clothes and sleeping in the bedding. None of them got ill.

Reed and his team now knew that infected bedding was not the answer to the question. They then turned to mosquitoes. They let mosquitoes bite sick patients in the hospital. Then those same mosquitoes bit healthy volunteers who were staying in the other house. Some of the volunteers caught yellow fever. One doctor even died from the disease.

## Science saves lives

The experiments proved that yellow fever is spread by mosquito bites. The US Army launched a campaign to kill off mosquitoes. Killing the mosquitoes in the area stopped the spread of the disease. Scientific enquiry and Reed's team saved the day!

DID YOU KNOW?

The doctors in Walter Reed's team experimented on people because no one knew of any animals that could get the disease. Some of Reed's team volunteered to be bitten. Most volunteers were soldiers. Their bravery saved thousands of lives.

## Ask questions and predict

Scientists ask questions and find the answers in a careful, orderly way. Reed did not just try different ideas until one worked; he had a plan. First he decided which question he was trying to answer: "How is yellow fever spread?" He learned everything he could about the disease.

Next, Reed predicted several possible answers to the problem. These predictions are called **hypotheses**. Reed had two hypotheses about the spread of yellow fever.

## Plan an investigation

Reed's team needed to test their hypotheses. They designed an experiment to prove whether people caught yellow fever from infected blankets and clothing. They planned another experiment to see if people caught the disease from mosquitoes. They had special houses built in which to conduct their experiments on volunteers.

Dr Walter Reed saved many lives by carefully testing his predictions until he found the right answer.

Yellow fever still exists in Africa, so mosquito nets are essential.

## Obtain, record, and present evidence

For the first experiment, mosquitoes were kept out of the house. That way, if the volunteers in the house got ill, Reed would know that it was the bedding and clothes, not the moquitoes, that caused it.

The second experiment was also controlled. Only mosquitoes that had bitten ill people were allowed in. Everything was kept very clean. These types of experiment are called **fair tests**. Reed's team wrote down details and kept careful records.

## Analyse the evidence and draw conclusions

When the results showed that mosquitoes spread yellow fever, more testing was done on other volunteers to make certain.

## Evaluate the investigation

Reed judged that he had proven that mosquitoes carried yellow fever. But where did the disease come from? More tests were needed. Later it was learnt that a **virus** actually causes the disease. The mosquitoes simply carry the virus from person to person.

DID YOU KNOW?

Mosquitoes breed in standing water. The army drained all **stagnant** bodies of water, or covered them with a layer of oil to kill the insects. Yellow fever had killed thousands of people in coastal cities in the United States. After Reed's discovery, yellow fever disappeared from the United States.

# Scientific enquiry

The word *science* comes from an old word, *scientia*, which means "to know". Science is a way to study the world around us. Science has been around for a long time, but new discoveries are still being made.

Science shapes the way we live today. The medicines we have, the cars and aeroplanes in which we travel, and the televisions and computers that we use were all developed with the help of science. Even the food you eat and the clothes you wear are products of science.

## A way of knowing

But what is science, exactly? Is it about mixing bubbling chemicals in test tubes? It can be, but often it is not. There are many ways of answering scientific questions, but this book focuses on **investigations**, where fair tests are used to test predictions. These predictions are known as hypotheses.

Space travel is possible because of scientific research.

**Scientific enquiry** has five important steps:

1. Ask questions and predict.
2. Plan an investigation.
3. Obtain, record, and present evidence.
4. Analyse the evidence and draw conclusions.
5. Evaluate the investigation.

Scientists do not always exactly follow this pattern. But Reed and his team used it to stop yellow fever. You can use it too.

**TRY IT!**

Around 800 years ago, people thought that rainbows were magical. A scientist called Roger Bacon did experiments to show that they were not. He found that a rainbow in the air is the same as the one you see in a water spray. Rainbows occur when tiny droplets of water in the air bend and **reflect** light. If the sun is shining behind you, you can make your own rainbows by spraying water from a hose or spray bottle.

# Research

If you have a question you want answered, scientific enquiry can help. The first step in this process is research. Find out what has already been learnt about the question you want answered. The chances are that you are not the first person to ask it.

Scientists build on the findings of other scientists. Like Walter Reed, you should complete your own careful research and **observation**. Observation means learning about things through your senses. Careful observation means looking at things in great detail.

## Observation tools

Scientific tools and equipment let us observe things that we otherwise could not. For example, **microscopes** help scientists examine organisms too tiny to see with our eyes alone. Remote controlled submarines explore the bottom of the ocean, acting as scientists' eyes, ears and hands down there. **Telescopes** allow us to see far out into the universe.

Scientists use high-tech microscopes to learn about tiny life forms.

The Hubble Space Telescope circles Earth and sends us photographs, so that we can learn more about space.

DID YOU KNOW?

An observer on Earth has to look at the night sky through air. Clouds, dust, and moving air make it hard to see clearly far into space. Telescopes above the air have a better view. The Hubble Space Telescope (HST) was launched in 1990. It is a powerful tool for space observation. It circles Earth from 600 kilometres (375 miles) above it. The HST has sent home amazing images of star births, star deaths, and worlds far away.

# Measurement

When scientists conduct experiments they often measure things. This helps them to observe more accurately. **Measurement** means finding the size or amount of something by comparing it to something else. We use tools, such as rulers and scales, to measure things.

## Recording

Taking careful notes is another important part of scientific enquiry. This is called recording. Measurements should always be recorded. Writing down observations and details of your experiments lets others see what you have learned. Photographs, video, sound recordings, and computers are tools for recording observations. Recording also allows other people to repeat your experiments.

# A brief history of science

People have always been curious about the world around them. When people in ancient times did not understand something, they often thought it was magic or the work of gods. Eventually, some people began to take a more logical approach. Maths and **astronomy** were developed in the Middle East and China more than 4,000 years ago.

## The Greeks

The ancient Greeks often thought like scientists. They asked serious questions about the world and tried to find practical answers. Aristotle lived more than 2,300 years ago. He used observation to find out for himself what was true.

Another Greek, Aristarchos of Samos, said that Earth moved around the Sun. He never tested this idea. Greek scientists did not always test things as scientists do now. Aristarchos' idea was not as popular as that of Ptolemy, another Greek. Ptolemy said that the Sun and planets moved around Earth. His **theory** was believed for 1,400 years.

The ancient Greeks believed in observing and finding facts. They did some experiments. They built on the knowledge of earlier people, but believed in checking things for themselves.

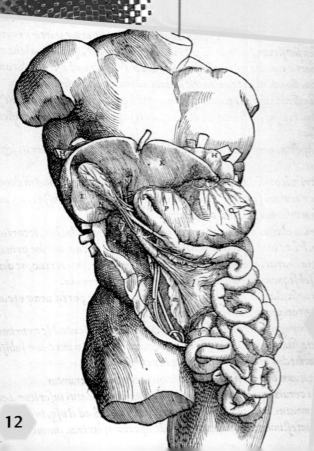

Andreas Vesalius was a Renaissance artist who studied dead bodies. His sketches helped others understand anatomy.

## The Dark Ages

From about AD 400 to 900, Europe sank into the Dark Ages. During this period, European people did not learn many new things. Meanwhile, in the Middle East, Arabic scientists translated many old Greek books, which prevented the work of the ancient Greeks from being forgotten.

## The Renaissance

Renaissance means "rebirth". This name was given to the time from about 1300 to 1527, when there was a rebirth of learning in Europe. In the 1400s a German printer named Johannes Gutenberg invented the printing press. As a result, books could be printed quickly and ideas could be shared. Old and new knowledge spread.

**DID YOU KNOW?**

Sir Francis Bacon (1561–1626) helped develop the process of scientific enquiry by teaching that scientists should experiment. It is thought that Bacon died after he caught a chill while doing an experiment. He wanted to see if stuffing a chicken with snow would keep it from rotting.

# A new way

In the past, scientists did not use scientific enquiry as we do today. For example, Aristotle was a great thinker in ancient Greece. He carefully observed and tried to check things for himself. But he also wrote things down that had not been proven by the kind of careful experiments scientists complete today. Sometimes Aristotle was wrong, but his work was so respected in Europe that even 1,000 years later, few people doubted what he had written.

Until the 1500s, **university** students were not supposed to question what Aristotle and other ancient thinkers had written. They were just supposed to memorize it. Experimenting and checking things were simply not done. But in the 1500s, things began to change. One man who made it change was Galileo Galilei.

As a student, Galileo was taught that heavier objects fall faster than light ones. Aristotle had said this was true. After all, we have all noticed a feather falls more slowly than a rock. But Galileo did not accept this. He rolled balls of different weights down a ramp. He compared how long it took them to reach the bottom. He proved the great Aristotle wrong.

This is a statue of the ancient Greek philosopher Aristotle.

# Falling objects

Galileo learnt that all things fall at the same speed unless **air resistance** comes into play. Air resistance is the pressure of air pushing against something. If there is no air in the way, a feather and a heavy object fall at the same speed. Astronauts have demonstrated this on the Moon, where there is no air.

Legend says that Galileo dropped balls from the Leaning Tower of Pisa in Italy to prove his hypothesis.

**TRY IT!**

Hold up a piece of paper and let it fall. It falls slowly because of air resistance. Take the same piece of paper and crumple it into a small ball. Let go and observe how it falls faster. It falls faster because it has less air resistance.

# Follow in Galileo's footsteps

You can try Galileo's experiment for yourself. Make sure you follow the steps of scientific enquiry.

**1 ❯ Ask questions and predict**

First, state the question you are trying to answer, "Does a heavy ball fall faster than a light one?" Then, think about your own observations. You have probably had experience with footballs, tennis balls, and others. Did the heavier ones seem to fall faster? Do research by looking up more information about Galileo's experiments. Your prediction should be based on observation and research. Galileo's hypothesis stated that a heavy ball and a light one fall at the same speed. You can use this hypothesis too.

**2 ❯ Plan an investigation**

Galileo rolled balls down a ramp because he could time them more easily. He said that rolling was like falling, but slower. He used wooden balls of different weights. You can drop different types of balls to see which falls faster.

**3 ❯ Obtain, record, and present evidence**

Stand on a chair with your arms raised and drop two balls of different weights. Be careful to let go of both at the same time. Watch them land.

Find balls that have different weights for your fair test.

You might need a partner to help you observe them landing. If possible try to use balls that are equally smooth on the outside. This might be difficult but it would make a better fair test. Like Galileo, you should repeat the test several times. As you test, record the number of times the heavy ball lands first. Record the number of times the lighter one lands first. Record the number of times they land together. A tally **graph** would be an easy way to keep track.

**4** **Analyse the evidence and draw conclusions**
After analysing his results, Galileo concluded that his hypothesis was correct. A heavy ball and a light one fall at the same speed. Do your results show this? They should!

**5** **Evaluate the investigation**
Galileo shared his findings with other scientists. Discuss and evaluate you results with others. Does anyone have any questions about your methods? Is there any way to improve the investigation?

Using your tally count, record your results in a clearly labelled bar chart.

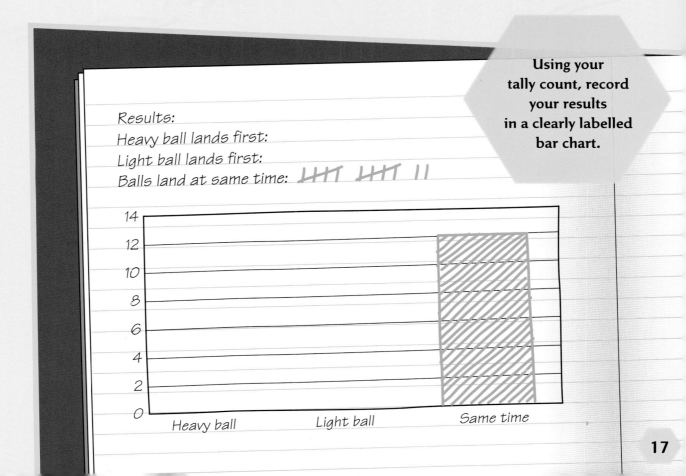

Results:
Heavy ball lands first:
Light ball lands first:
Balls land at same time: ⊬⊬⊤ ⊬⊬⊤ ‖

# The first modern scientist

Galileo was one of the first scientists to use scientific enquiry as we do today. When he wanted to find the answer to a question, he developed a hypothesis. Then he tested it with a fair test. He recorded his results and evaluated them, deciding if they proved or disproved his hypothesis. He tested things again to make sure his results were accurate. Many people consider him the first modern scientist.

## Tools for observation

Galileo is also important because he improved observations by using tools. Galileo invented one of the first thermometers to measure temperature. But probably the most important science tool Galileo taught scientists to use was the telescope.

In 1608 a Dutch **lens** grinder put two lenses inside a tube. This was the first telescope. Galileo soon built a stronger telescope. He was the first person to use a telescope to observe space.

Galileo Galilei helped to develop many scientific tools that are still used today.

# Pendulum clocks

Galileo was always asking questions. Once, when he was sitting in church, he looked at a lamp hanging from the ceiling. It swung back and forth. Nobody had watches back then and clocks were not very accurate, so he used his **pulse** as a kind of stopwatch. He measured how long each swing took. As the lamp began to settle into place, the swings grew smaller. But he noticed it still took the same amount of time for each swing.

The lamp had acted like a **pendulum**. Galileo made pendulums with materials of different **masses** and different lengths of string. He tested the pendulums to find out as much as he could about how they worked.

Galileo was the first person to see the moons of Jupiter.

DID YOU KNOW?

Galileo used his telescope to discover the four largest moons of Jupiter. They are called the Galilean moons after him. Their names are Io, Europa, Ganymede, and Callisto.

# Galileo's pendulum experiments

You can try Galileo's pendulum investigations to discover what changes the rhythm of a pendulum's swing. You can use a stopwatch to time the swings instead of your pulse.

**1** **Ask questions and predict**
Your question can be the same one Galileo asked 400 years ago: "How do you increase the number of swings a pendulum makes in 15 seconds?" You could predict that changing the weight of the pendulum, the length of the string, or the angle of release will work. These are three hypotheses.

**2** **Plan an investigation**
Your hypotheses can be tested in three separate fair tests. You can make a pendulum from string and metal washers. Cut a length of string and tie a small loop at each end. Fit one loop over a pencil. Tape the pencil to a desktop or table with half of the pencil over the edge of the desk. Poke a paper clip through the loop at the other end. Use this to hang washers or other weights.

**3** **Obtain, record, and present evidence**
Now you have a pendulum. Try three different tests. In each fair test, only one **variable** should change.

Work with a partner to conduct each of your three fair tests. One partner can be the timer. The other partner can count the swings. Do not push the pendulum. Just let it go. After 15 seconds, the timing partner can say, "Stop!" Record the number of swings.

1. First, use different weights on the pendulum.
2. Next, release the pendulum from different angles.
3. Finally, try different lengths of string.

Record your results in a graph or table.

**4** **Analyse the evidence and draw conclusions**
Which fair test produced the most swings in 15 seconds?
Do the results surprise you? Do any figures look out of place?

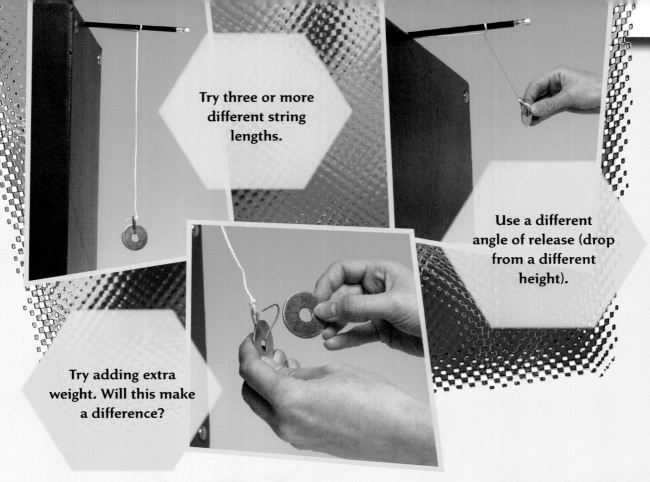

Try three or more different string lengths.

Use a different angle of release (drop from a different height).

Try adding extra weight. Will this make a difference?

⑤ **Evaluate the investigation**

Did you show that a shorter string increased the number of swings the pendulum makes in 15 seconds? If not, try to work out what went wrong!

A pendulum is any weight that swings back and forth. As you collect your results, record them in tables.

Different weights:

| Washers | Swings |
|---------|--------|
| 1 | 12 |
| 2 | 12 |
| 3 | 12 |

Changing the weight does not change the number of swings.

Different angles:

| Angle | Swings |
|-------|--------|
| high | 12 |
| medium | 12 |
| low | 12 |

Changing the angle does not change the number of swings.

Different lengths:

| Length | Swings |
|--------|--------|
| short | 19 |
| medium | 12 |
| long | 9 |

Changing the length changes the number of swings.
A short pendulum swings faster.

# Other scientists, other methods

Not all scientists after Galileo followed the fair test method of completing experiments. Even so, some of them moved science forward. In the 1600s Sir Isaac Newton explained how planets and moons move in space. He based much of his work on mathematics.

Another scientist in the 1600s, Anton van Leeuwenhoek (pronounced "lay-ven-hook"), discovered microbes with a homemade microscope. Microbes are microscopic living things. Van Leeuwenhoek was not following a fair-test experiment, but he was recording and communicating careful observations.

Carolus Linnaeus helped science by setting up a **classification** system for plants and animals in the 1700s. Linnaeus did not conduct experiments, but he organized information so that it could be understood better.

## Edward Jenner

By the 1700s many people were using scientific enquiry. One of them was Edward Jenner, who lived in England at a time when smallpox was common. Smallpox was a dangerous disease. It killed many of its victims and left its survivors covered with scars.

Edward Jenner is shown vaccinating a young boy with cowpox.

People who milked cows often caught a disease called cowpox. Cowpox was milder than smallpox and less dangerous. Jenner heard farmers say that people who caught cowpox did not get smallpox. He decided to investigate and find out if this was true.

Jenner put some liquid from a cowpox sore into a cut in a healthy boy's arm. The boy came down with a mild case of cowpox, but he recovered. Some weeks later Jenner gave the boy some liquid from a smallpox sore. The boy did not get smallpox. Jenner followed this with many more experiments and careful observation. Later, he published his results. Others started giving people cowpox in this way to save them from smallpox.

The results of Jenner's work are still being used today. Babies are vaccinated to protect them against illness.

**DID YOU KNOW?**

Jenner's idea spread around the world. His treatment came to be called *vaccination*. It is based on the Latin word *vacca*, which means "cow", as in cowpox. People no longer get vaccinated for smallpox because Jenner's **vaccine** stamped out the disease. But children today do receive vaccinations for other diseases such as measles, mumps, and rubella.

# Gregor Mendel

Gregor Mendel lived in Austria in the 1800s. He researched **genetics** – the study of the passing of **traits** from parents to offspring. Traits are things like eye and hair colour that you get from your parents. In plants, a trait might be the colour or shape of a flower, the size of a plant, or the juiciness of a fruit.

Mendel was a monk who looked after the monks' garden. They grew vegetables to eat, and he wanted to improve their crops. He wanted to know if there were patterns of traits being passed from parent plants to new plants. If Mendel could find these patterns, he could pick good traits and make them occur more often in new plants. That way, he could improve the crops. His hypothesis was that there were patterns of traits being passed down. He decided to find them.

Gregor Mendel did
many experiments

Dolly the sheep was a famous genetic clone.

## Cloning

Another example of scientific enquiry's impact on our lives can be found in genetics. One development in that field is cloning, the making of a new animal that is a copy of the parent. Scientists start cloning from a cell taken from the parent animal.

Animals are hard to clone. Scientists first tried cloning frogs in the 1950s. They have done countless experiments, using scientific enquiry to test many ways of cloning animals. They learnt something from each experiment. Finally, in 1996, scientists cloned a sheep named Dolly. They have since cloned mice, monkeys, pigs, and a cat.

**TRY IT!**

Plants have been cloned for hundreds of years. Cutting a piece from a plant and growing a new plant from it is cloning. You can clone a begonia or coleus plant. Cut some stem and a leaf off and plant it in some compost. If it grows, you have a genetic copy of the old plant – a clone.

# Science improves lives

Scientific progress over the last century has been amazing. Scientists are working to understand our world – in space, under the sea, in deserts and rainforests, at volcanoes, and in labs. They are finding ways to save animals, fight diseases, feed the world's people, reduce **pollution**, and make the world a better place.

Scientists make our world safer by testing different car designs using crash dummies. They crash them over and over again to come up with the safest car designs. Scientists also use scientific enquiry to solve crimes. They use microscopes and genetic evidence to help them catch criminals.

Scientists have learnt how to capture the energy from wind with turbines, and turn this energy into electricity.

**DID YOU KNOW?**

Some scientists dream of bringing back animal species that are **extinct**. They have collected genetic material from a woolly mammoth found frozen in the ice in Siberia. Mammoths became extinct around 10,000 years ago. Some scientists hope that they will be able to grow a cloned mammoth one day.

# Finding cleaner energy sources

Scientific enquiry is being used to find clean, safe ways to power our cars and heat and light our homes. One possible solution scientists are testing is hydrogen-powered cars. If cars run on hydrogen instead of gas, they do not pollute the air. The only thing that comes out of the exhaust pipe is a small amount of water.

Scientific enquiry is used every day to solve the world's problems. Scientists are testing better ways to use wind and ocean waves and sunlight to make electricity. These new methods are clean. We will never run out of wind, waves, and sunlight.

Scientific enquiry is even used in space to find out about the effects of weightlessness, and to test the soil on Mars.

# Testing things out

Professional scientists use scientific enquiry every day. You can use it too. Ask questions. Find out what others have already learnt. Then make a hypothesis. Design a fair test. Obtain evidence, making sure you control the variables so that only one thing causes the results. Take notes and keep careful records. Measure things. Analyse the evidence. What does it tell you? Does a pattern show up? Was your hypothesis correct? Evaluate the investigation and decide if you need to test anything else or use a different method. Think up new questions, hypotheses, and experiments. That is the scientific way of learning.

## Do you already use it?

You may already use scientific enquiry without realizing it. For example, you may ask yourself, "Why isn't the remote control working?" You make a prediction, such as, "The batteries are dead." You take them out and try new ones. Still not fixed? Maybe the television is unplugged. You check on that. You test hypotheses one by one until you find the answer.

If something is not working, you need to form hypotheses and test them one by one to discover the reason for the problem.

# Using scientific enquiry

You can use scientific enquiry to make your own life better. Can you change your morning routine so you get ready for school in less time?

Remember the steps of scientific enquiry. First, observe and ask questions. Do you spend a long time using the hairdryer? Could you shorten that time by air-drying your hair while you eat breakfast, then finishing it with the dryer? Make hypotheses. Plan and conduct fair tests. Write down how long it takes to do things in a different order or in different ways. Make sure you repeat each fair test more than once. Record and communicate your results. See if your results support your hypothesis. Then evaluate your investigations.

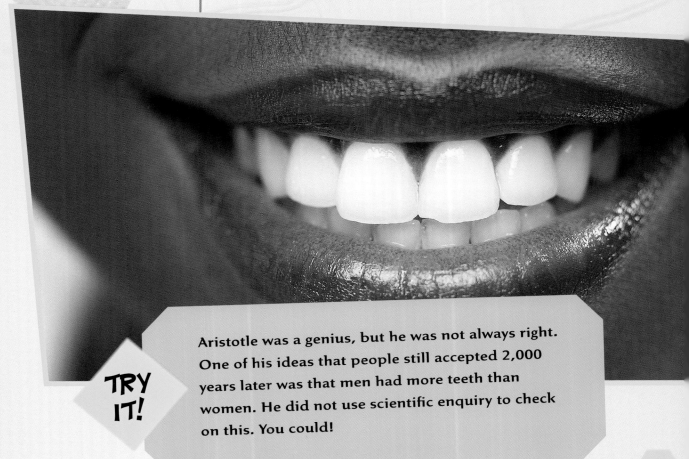

**TRY IT!**

Aristotle was a genius, but he was not always right. One of his ideas that people still accepted 2,000 years later was that men had more teeth than women. He did not use scientific enquiry to check on this. You could!

# Plants and music

You do not have to be a professional scientist to use scientific enquiry. You too can ask questions about the world around you. Your question could be, "Do plants grow taller if they are exposed to music?"

**1 Ask questions and predict**

To answer this question, you would need to read about plants. You would need to know about how plants grow. You would try to find information on music's effect on plant growth. You learn that light can affect a plant's growth. You predict that sound can affect a plant's growth too. Your hypothesis is that music will make the plants grow taller.

**2 Plan an investigation**

Plan a fair test so that you can be sure what caused the outcome. You would need to test lots of plants. If only one plant was used and it grew badly or died, there would be no way of being sure why this had happened. You need to play some plants music, and compare their growth with plants that do not get music.

A variable is anything that might affect the results of a fair test. An independent variable is something that may affect a dependent variable. Music is an **independent variable** that may affect a plant's growth. The growth is the **dependent variable.**

Think of everything else that could affect the growth of plants. All the plants must get the same water, sunlight, and soil. Even the pots used for planting must be the same. Use the same type of plant. Test only one variable. This means that everything should be the same for each plant except the music. Controlling all the other variables is the only way that you can be sure that, if the plants grow differently, it was the music that made the difference.

Measure the plants carefully and record the figures.

3 **Obtain, record, and present evidence**
Some of the plants should get music and some should not. Stick to one kind of music, in case it makes a difference. Check the plants regularly and measure their growth. Display your results on a graph or chart.

4 **Analyse the evidence and draw conclusions.**
According to your evidence, did the plants with music grow differently?

5 **Evaluate the investigation**
Do you think your results are reliable? Do any measurements stand out? If the plants with music grew better, perhaps the next step is to find out if plants prefer classical music or pop.

We need measurements because sometimes our eyes and minds fool us. Look at these lines. Which is longer? Now measure them with a ruler. Were you surprised?

# Birds and birdseed

When you choose a question to investigate, make it one that you can prove an answer to. Say you enjoy having birds in your garden. You plan to feed them and want to know what kind of seeds the birds like best.

**1 Ask questions and predict**

First find out about the birds that visit your garden. Try the Internet, the library, and asking anyone who might know. Learn what you can about the available seed mixes for wild birds. Then go to a shop and pick two or three brands of birdseed. Read the information on the packets. From the information you read, which birdseed do you predict that they will like best? Your hypothesis might be that they prefer Brand B. This is something you could prove or disprove. It is a statement you can test.

**2 Plan an investigation**

Plan a fair test to prove your hypothesis right or wrong. Make it a controlled experiment. To do this, keep everything the same except for the brand of birdseed. Any other variable that could affect the outcome must be the same for it to be a fair test.

Find the best birdseed to attract wild birds.

## 3 Conduct the fair test

Use measurements. You could weigh the birdseed or measure it another way. Put equal amounts out in the morning and measure what is left at night. Subtract to find out how much they ate. Keep records. Photographs and video would be useful, as well as written records. Repeat the experiment for several days.

## 4 + 5 Analyse the evidence, draw conclusions, and evaluate the investigation

After you analyse your results, your conclusion might be that your hypothesis was proven correct. Or maybe it was proven incorrect. You may decide that more testing or a different fair test is needed. Then, if you are being a good scientist, let others know about your findings so that they can copy your experiment.

Which brand do the birds like best? Have they liked this brand best throughout the investigation?

Results: Amount of birdseed eaten (in grams)

|  | Brand A | Brand B | Brand C |
|---|---|---|---|
| Day 1 | 120 | 95 | 110 |
| Day 2 | 160 | 150 | 180 |
| Day 3 | 115 | 105 | 110 |
| Day 4 | 140 | 70 | 90 |

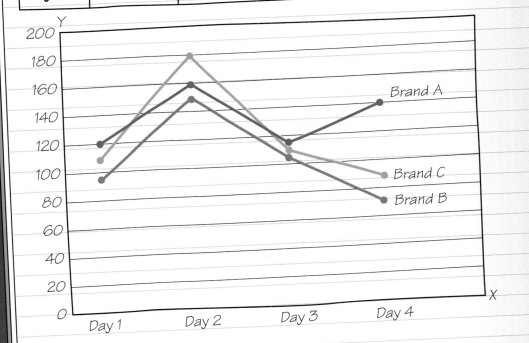

# Fast reflexes

In games, you notice that some of your friends have faster reflexes than others. You wonder if they were just born that way or if practice has made their reflexes faster.

**1 Ask questions and predict**

You ask a question such as, "Does practice make someone react more quickly when trying to catch a ruler?" Do you think that people will react more quickly with practice? You could research it. You predict that reaction time in catching a ruler will improve with practice. This is your hypothesis.

**2 Plan an investigation**

You need to think of a way to time a person's reactions. You decide to drop a ruler for someone to catch. The markings on the ruler will show you how quickly they caught it. By making several drops, you can see if reaction time improves. You would need to test several people to see if the results are the same for everyone. You will need to hold the ruler at the same height each time. The person you are testing sits and holds his or her catching hand at the same height each time.

Record the centimetre number under the hand that catches the ruler.

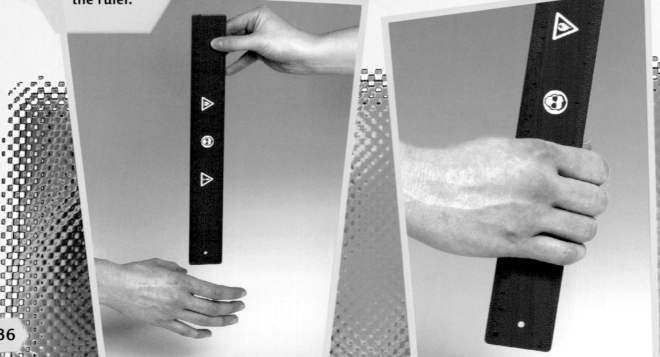

**TOP TIP**

In school you are used to having right and wrong answers to questions. But in science, it is fine if your hypothesis was wrong. You have not failed. You have still learned something.

**3 > Obtain, record, and present evidence**

Stand up and hold a ruler by the end that says 30 cm. You drop the ruler without warning. The person tries to grab it as quickly as possible. Record the centimetre marking where the hand catches the ruler. Do this several times. Then test someone else. Write down the measurements for all the testers. Present the results in a graph.

**4 > Analyse the evidence and draw conclusions**

Was your hypothesis correct? Did the people you tested tend to have either fast or slow reactions, or did they vary? Can you be sure that anyone's reactions improved with practice?

Lots of tests may be needed to get clear results.

**5 > Evaluate the investigation**

Can you think of ways to improve the fair test? Do you have more questions to answer? For example, if practice improves reaction time for catching a ruler, does it mean that practice will also improve other reflexes?

Results (in centimetres):

| Tester | 1st attempt | 2nd attempt | 3rd attempt |
|---|---|---|---|
| 1 | 27 | 15 | 5 |
| 2 | 18 | 16 | 14 |
| 3 | 17 | 26 | 1 |
| 4 | 20 | 3 | 28 |
| 5 | 20 | 18 | 9 |

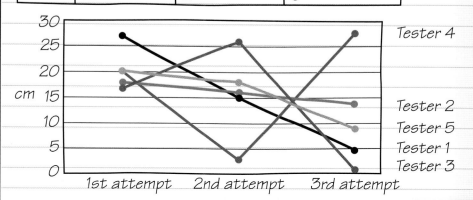

# Floating boats

Have you ever wondered why a boat floats? Is it because it is made of material that floats?

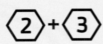

**1 Ask questions and predict**

You may have observed that some boats are made of wood and you know that wood floats. But you have also seen ships made of steel. You have observed that most steel objects sink. So what makes a boat float? Because you have noticed that boats all have a similar shape, you hypothesize that the shape of a boat makes it float.

**2 + 3 Plan an investigation and obtain, record, and present evidence**

You decide to choose a material and test several different shapes. Fill a bowl with water. Drop a lump of modelling clay in the water. Does it sink? Try shaping the clay in different ways to see if it will float. Repeat to be certain. Record your results for each shape. Write up your results and display them in a chart.

Even huge metal ships can float. How is this possible?

Test a boat shape, a ball, and other shapes.

**(4) Analyse the evidence and draw conclusions**

You discover that clay formed into a boat shape floats, and so does a bowl shape. Other shapes and lumps all sink. Based on your results, you conclude that it is the shape of a boat that makes it float.

**(5) Evaluate the investigation**

You have answered your question but you decide to do further research about buoyancy. Buoyancy means the ability to float.

You have noticed that people seem to be lighter in water. Buoyancy depends on how **dense** an object is. If two things are the same size, the one that weighs more is denser. If an object is denser than water, it sinks. A piece of clay is heavier than the amount of water that takes up the same space. But if you shape it like a boat, it is lighter. This is because the inside of a boat or ship is full of air. It is the same amount of clay, but it fills a larger space because it is hollow. The boat shape and the air in it together weigh less than the same volume of water. So a boat-shaped object floats, even if it is made of steel.

# Other investigations

By now you have learned enough about scientific enquiry to design your own investigations. What else could you investigate?

**1 > Ask questions and predict**
Some people are right-handed and some are left-handed. You ask if your cat is right- or left-pawed. You would start your scientific enquiry by observing cats and reading about them. You know most people are right-handed. You predict that most cats will be too. This is your hypothesis.

**2 + 3 > Plan an investigation and obtain, record, and present evidence**
You decide to see which paw a cat uses to bat a toy. How many cats should you test? Should you test each cat more than once? What variables need to be controlled? Record information as you go.

**4 + 5 > Analyse the evidence, draw conclusions, and evaluate the investigation.**
Did the results show a pattern? Was your hypothesis proven correct? Even if it was not, you have still learned something scientifically. It may lead you to do further research or investigations.

### 1 Ask questions and predict

Which gum's flavour lasts longest? Some brands claim theirs lasts longer. Can you investigate and find out? Base your hypothesis on advertising. You might choose Brand X because its advertising claims that it has long-lasting flavour.

### 2 + 3 Plan an investigation and obtain, record, and present evidence

You decide to test two kinds of gum, Brand X and Brand Y. You will need people who can time each other. How will you decide when the flavour runs out? Should the same people test both types of gum? Should the testers know which type of gum they are chewing? Display the results on a chart.

### 4 + 5 Analyse the evidence, draw conclusions, and evaluate the investigation.

Which brand's flavour lasted longer? Do the results support your hypothesis? Is there anything you could change to make the fair test better?

**Design your own experiments. What questions do you want to answer?**

*Which brand's flavour lasts longer?*
*Brand X:* | | | |
*Brand Y:* ‖‖‖‖‖‖‖‖
*Both the same:* | |

Same
2

Brand X
4

Brand Y
15

# Moving forward

Science is a way to learn about the world. Scientific enquiry is a way to find the answers to questions. Now that you have read this book, you should have a pretty good understanding of scientific enquiry and be able to use it.

You can read books to learn about animals, the stars, rocks, and anything else your curiosity leads you to. What do you find interesting? One famous fossil expert loved finding fossils and learning about dinosaurs as a kid. He never grew out of it. Now he makes a living digging up dinosaur bones.

## Science careers

There are several branches of science you could learn more about. Many different jobs exist in all these branches. Scientific enquiry is useful in all of them. Lots of other careers are not in the science field, but they use the scientific method.

Are you interested in the stars and planets? There is still much to learn in the field of astronomy. Did you know that new comets are still being discovered? Astronauts are scientists too.

Where will your curiosity lead you?

There are many different types of scientists. You could become one yourself.

Maybe you are interested in volcanoes and earthquakes. New things are being learned about the planet beneath our feet every year. Many exciting things are happening in plant and animal science. Researchers are developing new plants to feed the world's hungry people. There are many careers in medicine.

## Science in everyday life

You can also use scientific enquiry in your everyday life. It is a wonderful way to solve problems and learn about the world. Let your curiosity be your guide. That is how to be a scientist!

**TOP TIP**

Every library has a science book section. Look in the non-fiction part of the library. Ask the librarian where the science books can be found.

# Scientific enquiry flowchart

## ASK QUESTIONS AND PREDICT

Pick a topic and carry out some research. Think of a question you could answer by experimenting. The hypothesis is a statement that you can test. What do you predict will happen?

## PLAN AN INVESTIGATION

Which two variables will be the focus of your investigation? Plan how you will change one and measure and record how this affects the other. The other variables should be kept the same.

## OBTAIN, RECORD, AND PRESENT EVIDENCE

Carry out your investigation and observe carefully. Take and record exact measurements. Control the other variables in the fair test. Test things more than once. Choose a method to present your results clearly.

## ANALYSE THE EVIDENCE AND DRAW CONCLUSIONS

What does the data show? Are there any patterns or strange results? Were your predictions right?

## EVALUATE THE INVESTIGATION

The evaluation is where you decide how well your investigation worked. Even if your hypothesis was proved wrong, you have still learned something. Would a different method have worked better? Has the evidence made you ask more questions? If so, you can start a new investigation.

# Timeline of discovery

**2500 to 500 BC**  Astronomy begins in China and the Middle East

**500 BC to AD 500**  Ancient Greeks ask questions and think things happened because of natural causes, not the gods. They separate science from superstition.

**AD 500 to 1500**  Arabic people in the Middle East preserve the science of the ancient Greeks. The Dark Ages occur in Europe and not much progresses there at this time.

**1500 to 1700**  The Renaissance ("rebirth") of knowledge in Europe and the scientific revolution continues. The printing press spreads knowledge. Galileo uses modern scientific enquiry in the late 1500s and early 1600s. Galileo does pendulum experiments in the 1580s. The telescope and microscope are invented. Sir Isaac Newton uses mathematics to explain how objects move in space and on Earth. Van Leeuwenhoek discovers tiny living things with his microscope.

**1700 to 1800**  Experimentation occurs in many areas. Linnaeus organizes a classification system to group plants and animals. Jenner experiments with a smallpox vaccine.

**1800 to 1900**  Mendel studies inheritance in plants. Edison perfects the electric light bulb in 1879.

**1900 to present**  Walter Reed controls yellow fever in 1901. Astronomers study the universe. Spacecraft explore the solar system. Cloning is advanced. Medicine makes huge strides. Computers, television, radio, and robots are developed. Scientists study clean energy sources such as hydrogen.

# Glossary

**air resistance**  pressure of air pushing against something

**astronomy**  study of planets, stars, moons, and other things in space

**classification**  grouping of things by how they are alike

**dense**  heavier than another object of the same size

**dependent variable**  the variable (e.g. a plant's growth) that will be affected if you change the independent variable (e.g. amount of water)

**experiment**  careful test to see if a hypothesis is correct

**extinct**  having all died out

**fair test**  changing one variable at a time in an experiment while keeping everything else the same

**fertilize**  when a male makes a female plant or animal able to create offspring, seeds, or fruit

**genetics**  study of the passing of traits from parents to offspring

**graph**  diagram that shows the relationship between numbers

**hypothesis (more than one are called hypotheses)**  answer to a question that can be tested by doing an experiment

**independent variable**  the variable that you will change (e.g. amount of water), so that you can tell the effect that this has upon the dependent variable (e.g. the plant's growth)

**investigate**  use scientific enquiry to learn something

**lens**  piece of clear material curved on one or both sides to bend light passing through it

**mass**  measurement of the amount of matter contained in an object

**measurement**  finding the size or amount of something by comparing it to something else

**microscope**  device that makes tiny things look larger, usually by using lenses

**observation**  learning with your senses, especially by seeing

**pendulum**  hanging weight that can swing freely back and forth

**pollen**  male part of plant that fertilizes female part

**pollution**  harmful chemicals or waste in the water or air

**scientific enquiry** scientific way of finding things out, usually following these steps: asking questions and predicting; planning an investigation; obtaining, recording, and presenting evidence; analysing the evidence and drawing conclusions, and evaluating the investigation

**stagnant** not flowing, foul from standing still

**telescope** instrument that makes far-off objects look closer

**theory** explanation of how or why something happens, based on scientific study

**trait** characteristic that a plant or animal gets from its parents

**university** school of higher education

**vaccine** injection or something swallowed that contains dead or weakened germs to protect against a disease

**variable** something that can be changed in an experiment

**virus** extremely tiny thing that can cause disease

# Further reading

*Forces and Motion*, Peter Lafferty (Raintree, 2001)

*Galileo*, Paul Mason (Heinemann Library, 2001)

*Materials*, Chris Oxlade (Hodder Wayland, 2002)

*The Science of Forces*, Steve Parker (Heinemann Library, 2005)

# Index

# Titles in the *How to Be a Scientist* series include:

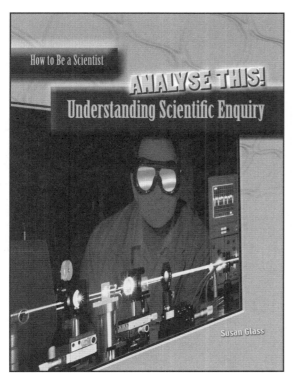

Hardback          978 0 431 90677 5

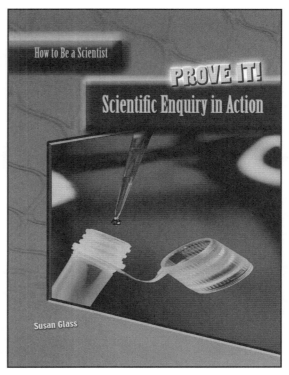

Hardback          978 0 431 90678 2

Hardback          978 0 431 90679 9

Find out about other titles from Heinemann Library on our website www.heinemann.co.uk/library

DID YOU KNOW?

By choosing a trait that is useful and breeding more plants with that trait, scientists have been able to improve crops. Many more people can be fed because crops have been improved.

# Pea plants

Over many years Mendel experimented with pea plants. Pea plants each have two parent plants. **Pollen** from one parent plant **fertilizes** the other plant. Then seeds for new plants are formed. Each parent passes on traits to the new plants.

Mendel carefully crossed tall plants with other tall ones, tall ones with short ones, and short ones with short ones. He measured the plants that grew from their seeds. He grew many generations to see how many became tall and short. He kept careful records. He studied around 28,000 pea plants!

Mendel's results showed there were patterns of traits being passed down from generation to generation. He learned that some traits were dominant. Dominant traits seem to overpower other traits. His hypothesis was correct. Plant growers and scientists could choose useful plant traits and breed plants with those traits.

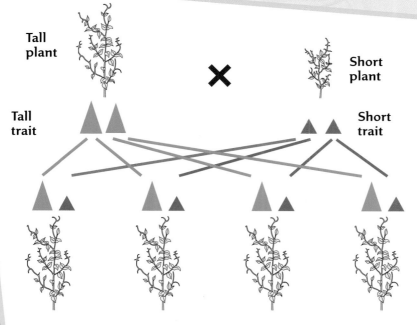

Tall plant

Short plant

Tall trait

Short trait

When tall pea plants are crossed with short ones, the offspring are tall.

All offspring are tall, proving that tall is the dominant trait.

# Modern science

During the past 300 years, science has made huge advances. Scientific enquiry has brought us electricity, radios, telephones, films, cars, planes, and spaceships. Scientific enquiry helps to unlock the secrets of Earth and space.

Science is applied to almost every part of our lives. Microwaves, computers, televisions, CDs, DVDs, medicines, and even clothing and food are all products of scientific enquiry.

## A bright idea

As one example, just think of all the ways you use electricity. Take the light bulb. Around 120 years ago, people lit their houses with gas lamps. Before that, they used candles. Thomas Edison invented the light bulb. His question was, "How can we use electricity to provide light?" His hypothesis was that he could find a material that would glow but not burn out quickly if an electric current ran through it.

He experimented and experimented. He worked five long years testing hundreds of kinds of fibres. Finally, he found one that worked!

Seattle's city lights show Edison's invention at work.